WHY BITCOIN

IS BITCOIN THE SOLUTION

TO A FLAWED SYSTEM?

Chris A. McLaughlin

Why Bitcoin - Written by Chris A. McLaughlin.

Why Bitcoin – The goal of this book is to educate people on Bitcoin. It is not intended as financial advice. When people first encounter Bitcoin it is usually met with interest based on its price, or scepticism based on its price. This book should help readers understand Bitcoin for more than its price, to be able to draw the conclusion of why Bitcoin was created, and to understand why Bitcoin has the potential to change the way we think about our current financial systems. The book is intended to be short and snappy in some parts and philosophical and thought-provoking in other parts.

I aim, where possible, to keep the chapters under 5 minutes each. Although *'Why Bitcoin'* has technical elements, the intention is not to dive too deep into the intricacies of Bitcoin technology. The technical components are described with layman explanations where possible. The book is aimed to be inclusive to all levels and backgrounds. Bitcoin is a subject with deep layers that can only be understood with many hours of research.

I would like to give a special thanks to Thomas Moore for his input into this book, thanks to Ian Crawford for proofreading the book, and to thank my friends and family for supporting me throughout this journey.

And don't worry, the price of Bitcoin does have its own dedicated section in the book.

CONTENTS

Section 1: Understanding money 1

    What is Money 1

    The Properties of Money 5

    The Value of Gold 10

    The Flaws in Gold 14

    The Introduction of Fiat currency 17

Section 2: What is Bitcoin and Why Bitcoin was Created 23

    Satoshi Nakamoto 23

    What is Bitcoin 30

    Bitcoin Scarcity 34

    21 Million Bitcoin 37

    Proof of work 40

    The Bitcoin Halving and Supply 44

Section 3: Bitcoin Technology 53

    The Bitcoin Blockchain 53

    Bitcoin Mining and the Difficulty Adjustment 57

The Bitcoin Network of Nodes 63

Bitcoin Consensus 68

Wallets and Addresses 72

Section 4: The Emergence of Bitcoin 79

Analogue to Digital 79

Bitcoin vs Gold 87

Improvements on Gold's Flaws 91

Bitcoin Vs Fiat 93

The Bitcoin Price 100

Bitcoin Total Addressable Market (TAM) 111

Section 1

Understanding money

What is Money

I believe the best path to understanding Bitcoin is to first understand money, secondly, to understand the reasons why Bitcoin was created, and thirdly, to understand the technology that makes Bitcoin one of the most profound inventions in history. As price movements draw people in, people then often try to understand the technology but many fail to understand the economic impact of Bitcoin and its value in the world, both today and for the future. Understanding the 'why' behind Bitcoin is the most important step in the journey.

So, what is money? We often take money for granted and

don't question its origin. Money, like Bitcoin, is also an invention. Money as we know it today came in many different forms throughout history. If you think back to a time before physical and digital money, **how do you think goods and services were exchanged?**

Thousands of years ago, humans operated in a barter economy. A barter economy pre-dates the use of money. A barter economy is a cashless economic system in which services and goods are traded at negotiated rates.

A barter economy worked to a certain point, but one major hurdle was valuing one good against another. It wasn't easy to agree on a unit to measure all transactions

For example:

Are 3 fish equal to the value of 20 pineapples? Is a spear equal to the value of a pair of sandals?

Although if you were brave enough and you were the one with the spear, you could certainly craft ways to snatch the sandals!

Based on these examples, you can see how flawed the barter economy can be.

It isn't certain who invented money but eventually humans figured out that if there was a trusted unit system that had certain properties, it could be used to facilitate human-to- human transactions.

Some early versions of units used as money for transactions were things such as:

- Livestock
- Sand
- Salt
- Rocks
- Shells
- Metals

And many more.

In the next section we'll look at the properties that make good, sound money, along with why some of the early versions of money failed.

The Properties of Money

In this section we'll look at what makes good, sound money, and what doesn't. In the previous section, *what is money*, we showed examples of units which were used in exchange for goods and services.

- Livestock
- Sand
- Salt
- Rocks
- Sea Shells
- Metals

If we look at some of the **properties** that make good, sound money, and we ask ourselves whether these previous versions of money meet these desired properties, we'll soon discover why they eventually failed as money.

	Livestock	Sand	Salt	Rocks	Shells	Metals
Durable	D	B	C	B	C	A
Portable	D	C	C	C	C	C
Divisible	C	B	B	C	D	C
Recognizable	B	B	B	D	D	B
Scarce	D	D	B	D	D	B

The desirable properties of money can have many different attributes. We are going to focus on the 5 main properties which are desirable of money:

> Durability
>
> Portability
>
> Divisibility
>
> Recognizability
>
> Scarcity

Let's take a look at these desired properties and decide which previously used forms of money worked and which failed.

Durability – Money must be sturdy enough to stand the test of time. What happens to the durability of salt if it comes into contact with water? Is Livestock a good example of durable money? Cows won't be able to serve as money for hundreds of years due to their limited lifespans. However, some metals, if you dropped them to the bottom of the ocean and came back a thousand years later, would be in the same condition. It may be a wet lump of metal after doing this experiment but this is what gives metals strong durability and a potential for being money.

Portability – Money needs to be small, light, and easy to carry or transport. As a form of money, imagine the inconvenience of transporting live animals over a great distance. Transporting something like sand is much easier but in large quantities could prove to be problematic.

Divisibility – Money needs to be divisible so change can be given. Sand comes in small enough units that it doesn't necessarily need to be more divisible but sand may face the problem of each unit being too small. What if you tried to divide sea shells in to smaller units? Does fracturing the unit render the money worthless in this case?

Recognizability – Money needs to be recognisable and uniform, in certain ways, for it to be widely used. Grains of sand look similar at a glance so many would think it ticks the box on this property but sand can vary in different geographies and conditions. Rocks are flawed as recognisable money in a more obvious way, as rocks come in different shapes sizes and colours. Today, physical metal coins are recognisable by having been molded into identical shapes, sizes, and weight. Many producers of coins establish recognisability by having a 'stamp,' often a figure head carved in the coin. Examples include Queen Elizabeth, US presidents, a king, or a leader.

Scarcity – Money needs to be scarce, not easily created or produced. If cows were today's form of money, wouldn't everyone be trying to breed as many cows as possible, and working on ways to speed up the farming of cows? Eventually an over-production of cows would take place and cows would become extremely abundant. In the basic fundamentals of economics, if supply outstrips demand, the value of the good or asset will decrease. On the other hand, certain metals are not easily found and unable to be recreated. Certain metals are scarce due to the difficulty to locate and produce them - More on this in a later chapter.

Given the properties required to be good, sound money, you can see why many of the early forms of money failed. From what we've learned so far, the form of money that best aligns to the desired propertied of money would be metals. We will find out in the next chapter which metal established itself as universally recognized money for thousands of years.

The Value of Gold

In the previous chapter, we looked at the properties of money and why metals best align with the desired properties of good, sound money. In this section we'll take a look at why, out of all the available metals, gold became the universally recognised form of money for more than five thousand years.

Silver was once a competitor for Gold as money since it has similar properties, but silver is lacking in key attributes when compared to Gold. Gold is durable to the point of virtual indestructibility. Gold doesn't rust and it isn't affected by time. Using the earlier example, if you dropped gold to the bottom of the ocean and came back a thousand years later, gold would be in the same condition. Other metals, like silver, can tarnish slightly over time, even if it is only slightly. Gold is non-reactive with chemicals. It doesn't corrode and always retains its colour.

Recognisability is a key property of money. Even today gold is distinctly different to many other metals. The colour of gold is quite unique and **recognisable.**

In any period throughout history, regardless of mechanics and technology, when it comes to **portability** and storage, a lighter metal is going to be easier to transport than a heavier metal. Silver is heavier than gold, and therefore it is generally more difficult to transport.

Gold is also more scarce than silver, meaning it is more difficult to locate and mine gold versus silver. Silver is scarce but in comparison to gold, it is more abundant. In general, assets that are scarce will carry more value than those with less **scarcity.**

With gold being the lighter metal and being more valuable due to its scarcity, it also became easier to store gold over silver – If you wanted to store one million dollars' worth of gold and silver, you would require less storage space when storing the same monetary value of gold than you would of silver.

With gold being more durable, recognisable, portable, and scarce than silver, it became the most widely adopted version of money. Silver has been used alongside gold in certain societies as a less valuable form of money than gold.

One of gold's best properties was the 'store of value' property, driven by its scarcity. People want to hold an asset for the long term without it depreciating. Using an example from today, we know that holding today's money over time will usually get you less value in the future. House prices for example have been increasing over time. In the early 1900's you could buy good property for $5000, in 2000 you could buy the equivalent house for $100,000, and today an equivalent house in 2022 could be $300,000 or more. Today's money doesn't hold value over time, more on that later.

In history, gold had the ability to hold value over time due to scarcity against goods – is it possible for today's money to become a store of value where you can store your wealth today, and can it buy you the equivalent good or service in the future without worrying about money losing its value?

If gold didn't exist, silver would have assumed the status as the most valuable form of money. Ultimately, the best form of money will eventually become the universally accepted form of money. In this case, historically, gold has been the best form of money known to mankind.

The Flaws in Gold

In the previous chapter we looked at how gold became the money of choice. Gold was the best form of money out of all previous forms of money for thousands of years. However, gold isn't perfect and has had its drawbacks in the past. Humans have previously reduced the amount of gold in gold coins by mixing other base metals into the coins. The results of this created more 'Gold mixed' coins which gave more money to those in power, for spending while it resulted in inflation for citizens. The more coins or units in circulation results in an increase of the price of goods and services.

Currency debasement in history is the process of reducing the amount of precious metal in coins and replacing them with cheaper base metals such as copper. This process has taken place many times in history to help fund wars and invasions for those who control the money supply.

Roman emperor Nero began debasing Roman currency around 60 AD by reducing its silver content from 100% to 90%. Over the next 150 years, the silver content was reduced to 50%. By 265 AD, the silver content was down to 5%. For Roman citizens, this resulted in an increase of money supply in society which, in turn, increased the cost of goods. The increased money supply meant there was **more money chasing the same goods**.

The final property of money that exposes a flaw in gold is gold's recognizability and verifiability. Gold is easily recognisable to the eye, but it isn't entirely verifiable. If someone brought you a gold bar today, without special equipment and a set of scales, you couldn't tell for certain that the entire gold bar is pure gold. The outer shell of the gold bar could be pure gold and the centre could be mixed with other metals.

Outside of the properties of money, there are other issues with gold being money.

Do you know how much gold there is in the world? The amount of gold that exists on earth isn't known. Isn't this a problem when determining scarcity?

Gold has also suffered from confiscation. It became illegal in the US for citizens to own gold bullion from 1933 to 1974. Although the government allowed people to exchange their gold at a reasonable price at the time, laws were introduced to seize gold from citizens had they not exchanged their gold for dollars. At the time of confiscation, the US dollar became the world reserve currency under the Bretton Woods agreement. The agreement meant all national currencies were valued in relation to the U.S. dollar. Gold was still used as money but not by citizens but by governments.

As perfect as gold was while it served its time as universally recognized money, it still had flaws – given the technology advances in the 21st century, **might there be an opportunity to improve on the properties of money?**

The Introduction of Fiat currency

Even with golds flaws, gold still became the best form of money available. Gold came in different forms but mainly as gold coins. As gold coins became widely adopted, as well as more valuable, storage became a challenge. As a result, people started storing their gold in more secure locations, like vaults. When a person would deposit their gold into a vault, the vault owners gave the person a receipt for the gold in storage. People could use these receipts in exchange for goods and services. This was the introduction of paper money – sort of like an I owe you (IOU). People could then go to the vault with the receipt and exchange it back to gold if they wanted, This is how banking started.

The paper money was **backed by gold,** meaning for every paper dollar given out by a bank, an equal amount of gold was present in a vault. This means that the dollar is backed 1:1 (one to one) with gold.

As things evolved in this manner, nations also started storing their wealth in gold in vaults. Governments linked the value of its paper money to its gold reserves – this is what is referred to as the **GOLD STANDARD.** Currencies were directly **pegged to gold.** At one point in time, most of the world's economies were basing their monetary system on the gold standard.

As examples, if Canada had a total money reserve of $100 Billion, it would mean that Canada should have $100 billion stored in gold in its vaults and if the UK had $500 Billion in money reserves, it would mean that the UK should have $500 billion stored in gold in its vaults. During the Gold Standard, the gold supply became the main controlling factor for the inflation, meaning the more gold produced resulted in an increase of the inflation of goods and services – There are other factors in economics to consider but as a broad measure and with all things being equal, if 2% more gold was found or produced through mining in a year, inflation would generally go up 2%, in line with this increase, which means the price of goods and services in an economy would increase by 2%. Gold functioned naturally as an inflation control due to its scarcity and difficulty to produce.

In 1971, during the American presidency of Nixon, the US, an economic superpower, ended its attachment to the gold standard. This meant a dollar bill was no longer redeemable for gold in the way it did before – the dollar was no longer backed 1:1 with gold. Paper money, the dollar, was then made legal tender in the US by order of the government- this form of money is referred to as '**Fiat' money**.

Fiat money is money issued by the government and regulated by a central authority or central bank. The word Fiat comes from the Latin word that means 'by decree', meaning by order. Essentially fiat is money that is legal tender **by order** of a government. Unlike money in during the Gold Standard, there is no backing to fiat money other than a government ordering it's citizens to use it.

The US was operating under the gold standard until 1971 and since 1971, the US dollar is operating as a fiat currency. The US dollar is under the control of the US central bank, the federal reserve (The Fed). Other examples of central banks are the Bank of England (BOE), the European Central Bank (ECB), Bank of Japan (BOJ) etc. These central banks also operate under the fiat system, where the central bank controls the money supply for a country or countries. With the US dollar being the world reserve currency, other countries were forced to come off the gold standard and adopt a fiat system.

As mentioned previously, the amount of gold that could be produced in any given period helped control inflation – What would happen if central banks could spin up their money printer and print up money out of thin air using a currency which isn't back by anything?

Summary of Section 1

In the section just covered, we asked the question: what is money? We explored the first forms of money. We looked at what are the properties of good sound money. We concluded why gold emerged as the best form of money for thousands of years. We also outlined the inherent flaws in gold as money. We looked at the evolution of money from physical gold to paper money and the move to Fiat currency in the last century.

The next section will explain why Bitcoin was created and how it is designed to tackle some of the biggest problems in the economic world since the introduction of Fiat Money.

Why Bitcoin

Section 2

What is Bitcoin and Why Bitcoin was Created

Satoshi Nakamoto

Who is Satoshi Nakamoto?

One of the most interesting parts of Bitcoins history is the creator of Bitcoin - Satoshi Nakamoto. Satoshi Nakamoto is a pseudonymous name used by the person who first introduced Bitcoin to the world in public forums. It is still unknown who Satoshi is, even whether Satoshi is a man or a woman. Given the properties of Bitcoin, Satoshi had a deep understanding of money, computer science, mathematics, cryptography, economics, and human behavior.

Satoshi Nakamoto published the Bitcoin Whitepaper in 2008 and started communicating through online public forums, discussing Bitcoin in early 2009 before posting mainly on Bitcointalk.org in late 2009. Satoshi's last post on these forums was December 2010. During those 2 years Satoshi spent time explaining the concepts to others and working on improving the Bitcoin security and protocol.

Summary - satoshi	
Name:	satoshi
Posts:	575
Activity:	364
Merit:	2610
Position:	Founder
Date Registered:	November 19, 2009, 07:12:39 PM
Last Active:	December 13, 2010, 04:45:41 PM

Satoshi Nakamoto post summary - Bitcointalk.org

In that time, Satoshi had engaged with enough people to start building up the network, which created more security as more users joined the network. Satoshi had reservations about Bitcoin making it to mainstream media in the early days as there was still work to do during that time. This was evident when Bitcoin got attention from a

PC world article and WikiLeaks in 2010 highlighting the potential benefits of Bitcoin which drew a lot of attention to Bitcoin, which Satoshi didn't approve of the attention for such a new project. In retrospect, Satoshi may have known that if Bitcoin was to be compromised, it would be best for bad actors to do this while the network was in its infancy. Today, Bitcoin is the second largest computer network behind the internet but it is the most secure and most powerful computer network on the planet. It was important for the Bitcoin network to be protected in its early years in order for it to grow, organically, to a size that allowed the network to protect itself from attacks.

In late 2010, Satoshi disappeared from online forums, leaving Bitcoin in the hands of the community. Satoshi was the first miner of Bitcoin and mined around 1 million Bitcoin in total, which have never been spent or touched. These Bitcoin can still be located on the Bitcoin blockchain today for everyone to see – More on the blockchain later. Satoshi's unspent, mined Bitcoin is a testament of security of the network. Satoshi's Bitcoin, which are publicly known, are the largest bounty on the planet for hackers to try and crack, and no one has been able to move or spend these Bitcoin.

Satoshi had written a Whitepaper for Bitcoin and throughout the Bitcoin Whitepaper, Satoshi references **Trust** as a key weakness of financial institutions. Satoshi's intention was to design a system that would allow any two willing parties to transact directly with each other without the need for a trusted third party. Imagine if Bob could transfer money to Alice any time he wanted, without having to rely on an entity like a bank to verify and approve the transaction.

Is it a coincidence that Satoshi introduced Bitcoin during the great financial crisis in the 2000's? The very first block mined on Bitcoin, often referred to as the genesis block, has a reference written on it quoted from The Times newspaper headline in 2009 saying – 'Chancellor on brink of second bailout for banks' in reference to banks being bailed out during the financial crisis.

What is Bitcoin and Why Bitcoin was Created

```
00000000  f9 be b4 d9 1d 01 00 00  01 00 00 00 00 00 00 00  |................|
00000010  00 00 00 00 00 00 00 00  00 00 00 00 00 00 00 00  |................|
00000020  00 00 00 00 00 00 00 00  00 00 00 00 3b a3 ed fd  |............;...|
00000030  7a 7b 12 b2 7a c7 2c 3e  67 76 8f 61 7f c8 1b c3  |z{..z.,>gv.a....|
00000040  88 8a 51 32 3a 9f b8 aa  4b 1e 5e 4a 29 ab 5f 49  |..Q2:...K.^J)._I|
00000050  ff ff 00 1d 1d ac 2b 7c  01 01 00 00 00 01 00 00  |......+|........|
00000060  00 00 00 00 00 00 00 00  00 00 00 00 00 00 00 00  |................|
00000070  00 00 00 00 00 00 00 00  00 00 00 00 00 00 ff ff  |................|
00000080  ff ff 4d 04 ff ff 00 1d  01 04 45 54 68 65 20 54  |..M.......EThe T|
00000090  69 6d 65 73 20 30 33 2f  4a 61 6e 2f 32 30 30 39  |imes 03/Jan/2009|
000000a0  20 43 68 61 6e 63 65 6c  6c 6f 72 20 6f 6e 20 62  | Chancellor on b|
000000b0  72 69 6e 6b 20 6f 66 20  73 65 63 6f 6e 64 20 62  |rink of second b|
000000c0  61 69 6c 6f 75 74 20 66  6f 72 20 62 61 6e 6b 73  |ailout for banks|
000000d0  ff ff ff ff 01 00 f2 05  2a 01 00 00 00 43 41 04  |........*....CA.|
000000e0  67 8a fd b0 fe 55 48 27  19 67 f1 a6 71 30 b7 10  |g....UH'.g..q0..|
000000f0  5c d6 a8 28 e0 39 09 a6  79 62 e0 ea 1f 61 de     |\..(.9..yb...a.|
000000ff
```

The blockchain, which we'll cover in more detail soon, is an open transparent ledger with a record of every transaction ever made – Think of it as a public ledger. This message from Satoshi about bank bailouts is embedded on the Bitcoin blockchain forever. It may be a clue to the motivation behind the creation of Bitcoin.

To this date, Satoshi has not re-emerged or communicated in any form since disappearing from forums in 2010. Satoshi and the community made updates to the protocol during his active years on the forums and left the protocol in a condition where Bitcoin can survive hundreds, if not thousands of years, in its current condition. Satoshi being removed from the equation is another reason why Bitcoin has become a more decentralised asset. Having a central figure who can influence decisions leaves the protocol vulnerable and more open to being compromised.

There have been many suggestions who Satoshi Nakamoto is, with some also believing Satoshi is no longer alive. Whatever the reason, Satoshi wanted to remain anonymous forever. We may never discover who Satoshi is or was.

What is Bitcoin

Now that we've explored the topic and, thereby, have a better understanding of money, it's time to look at Bitcoin and try to understand why Bitcoin was created and what problems it was designed to solve.

Bitcoin is described in many ways by different people:

- An electronic peer-to-peer payment system

- A decentralised currency

- A digital ledger

- Digital gold

- The native currency of the internet

As we know, Bitcoin is a digital currency created in 2009 by Satoshi Nakamoto. Throughout history, previous attempts at creating digital currency have come and gone; B Money, Bit Gold and Hashcash to name a few. The idea of a neutral digital currency isn't new and has been about since the 1970's, possibly spurred on by the move to centralized money, fiat, in 1971. The main downfall of previous versions of decentralized digital currencies were having a single point of failure and having potential security flaws. We'll find out soon why Bitcoin excels in both these areas.

The Bitcoin whitepaper, which can be found online, was published by Satoshi Nakamoto in 2008 and describes Bitcoin as '**A purely peer-to-peer version of electronic cash that would allow online payments to be sent directly from one party to another without going through a financial institution.**'

As well as being a digital currency, Bitcoin can also be seen as a computer program, a protocol, and a network. Bitcoin was written in code as an **opensource protocol**, meaning the code is publicly accessible. This is important for transparency and trust in the protocol.

Bitcoin is also the currency of the Bitcoin network. Bitcoin can be transferred between users of the Bitcoin network without a centralized party. Another way of saying this is to say the Bitcoin network is Decentralized - Transactions are essentially permissionless and trust-less, allowing the network of nodes/computers to validate transactions rather than a central individual, group, or government. All transactions are recorded on a digital ledger that is verified by the network of users. At this point a curious question would be – who owns the node/computers that validate transactions? The answer to this question will help you understand why previous versions of digital currency have failed and why Bitcoin is succeeding. This is covered in the coming chapters.

In these next chapters, we'll dive into the economic properties of Bitcoin before engaging in the technology of Bitcoin. Explaining the properties of Bitcoin will naturally open up questions which will be addressed in later chapters. In order to get the best out of this section, it is wise to assume, for now, that the Bitcoin protocol and technical aspects of Bitcoin are sound - For example, assume it to be correct if a chapter states that there are currently only 21 million Bitcoin within the protocol. We'll discover what makes the protocol sound in our

Understanding Bitcoin Technology chapters, but first let's look at Bitcoins properties.

Bitcoin Scarcity

We covered scarcity being one of the desired properties of money in earlier chapters. If money was easy to extract or create, it is likely to loses value against money that is difficult to extract or create. Gold cannot be created from nothing, although humans have tried to do so through alchemy for many years without success. Gold cannot be easily taken from the ground, and it isn't an abundant asset. Gold is more scarce that many other metals, which is one of the key reasons it is the metal of choice when it comes to money.

There is no question that water and oxygen is more valuable to humans than gold, silver, and diamonds, but we value gold, silver, and diamonds as monetarily more valuable. The reason being is one is overly abundant and the other is scarce. Supply and demand both play a huge part in scarce assets. More on the demand side later.

How does Bitcoin compare in scarcity to other assets. Bitcoin has been programmed to only have 21 million Bitcoin. This makes Bitcoin a fixed supply asset. When you compare bitcoin to all other assets in history, it is the only asset that is truly scarce due to it being programmatically fixed.

With there being a fixed amount of Bitcoin, which does not increase past 21 million, do you think Bitcoin would be more or less valuable if Bitcoin had an increase in supply of 10% a year? With an increase in supply of 10% per year, Bitcoin would become less valuable against similar assets with an increase in supply of less than 10% a year. In the long term, desired assets with the least increase in supply will likely become more valuable than assets which have a faster increase in supply.

What if you could change the supply of an asset as you wish? Or what if you could create more supply of an asset through ingenuity? What if a new tool or technology is created that allowed humans to extract gold at a much higher rate than ever before? What happens if a mountain of gold, land under the sea or an asteroid with an abundance of gold is discovered and through technology is easily accessible – what happens to the price of gold in the long term if these scenarios are played out?

When you think of other assets that are as scarce as Bitcoin you have to think of valuable assets that cannot be recreated or are fixed in supply. You could say that a Picasso painting is the most scarce asset because Picasso is no longer alive, so more Picasso paintings cannot be produced, but because the locations and number of all Picasso paintings are not known, there could be more unaccounted for Picasso paintings discovered in the future, making the paintings less scarce and less valuable. Not knowing the potential supply of an asset puts scarcity at risk.

With Bitcoin being an **open-source** protocol and having a **programmatically fixed supply** of 21 million, it is provable that Bitcoin is the scarcest asset in history.

21 Million Bitcoin

As we've discovered, the Bitcoin protocol has been coded to contain only 21 million Bitcoin. A question people often ask is how 21 million Bitcoin will serve the entire population of the world as money. There are over 7 billion people on the planet but only 21 million Bitcoin.

A Bitcoin is the measurement of 1 whole unit within the Bitcoin protocol. What many don't understand is that Bitcoin can be divisible into fractions. Each Bitcoin can be broken in to one hundred million sub-units. These sub-units have been named by the community as 'Satoshi's' or 'Sats' for short – after the creator Satoshi Nakamoto. If you wanted to buy and own a tenth of Bitcoin, you can. Instead of acquiring 1 Bitcoin you can purchase 0.1 Bitcoin, you can purchase 0.01 Bitcoin, you can even purchase 0.000001 Bitcoin. You will often hear the Bitcoin community tell people how they like to accumulate Bitcoin by 'Stacking Sats', essentially buying more Bitcoin in fractions.

Just as Dollars can be broken into one hundred individual cents and 1 kilogram in to one thousand grams, Bitcoin can be broken in to one hundred million Sats. This gives Bitcoin greater divisibility. In fact, the entire number of Sats in the Bitcoin protocol is set at 2.1 quadrillion Sats – 21,000,000,000,000,000 Sats.

SATOSHI CONVERTER

1 Satoshi	= 0.00000001 BTC
10 Satoshi	= 0.00000010 BTC
100 Satoshi	= 0.00000100 BTC
1,000 Satoshi	= 0.00001000 BTC
10,000 Satoshi	= 0.00010000 BTC
100,000 Satoshi	= 0.00100000 BTC
1 million Satoshi	= 0.01000000 BTC
10 m Satoshi	= 0.10000000 BTC
100m Satoshi	= 1.00000000 BTC

It is logical that in the future, as Bitcoin becomes more widely adopted, people will speak in terms of Sats. Instead of saying a cup of coffee costs 0.000001 Bitcoin, you can simply say a cup of coffee costs 100 Sats - 0.00000100

Bitcoin is the same as 100 Sats.

After understanding Sats, more questions usually arise. What if 2.1 quadrillion isn't enough to serve the entire population of the world? Because Bitcoin is code, Bitcoin can technically be infinitely divisible. More divisibility doesn't mean creating more Bitcoin: it means the pieces or fractions can become smaller. Technically gold is divisible to the size of an atom but we usually only measure fractions of gold in ounces and grams.

Sats can be divided into smaller units. Currently, subdivisions of Sats are not widely spoken about but, this may be needed and we could refer to these units as NanoSats or MicroSats as an example. Bitcoin is currently calculated to 8 decimal points but can be moved to 16 decimal points if required.

Proof of work

Proof of work is a key component of the Bitcoin network. This is a technical section of the book and is simplified to help understand the concept.

As mentioned in the properties of money chapter, being able to create or produce an asset easily can lead to the over-production of an asset and eventually lead to devaluation.

Since the first Bitcoin block was produced in 2009, Bitcoin is slowly released by the protocol in increments until the 21 million limit is reached. New Bitcoin is released into the system roughly every 10 minutes. In the protocol, Satoshi used an existing cryptography algorithm (SHA-256) which requires computers to use computing power to solve a cryptographic puzzle or in simple terms, guessing a randomized number (Hashing). Whoever guesses this random number is rewarded with an increment of Bitcoin, referred to as the block reward. The computers that solve these problems are normally referred to as miners.

Satoshi Nakamoto recognised that it is important that the new supply of bitcoin shouldn't be easy to produce and obtain. The Solution: In order to produce new Bitcoin, energy must be spent. The solution to Satoshi's problem, ensuring that energy was to be used to produce new Bitcoin, is referred to as the **proof of work** mechanism – The Proof of Work mechanism ensures miners expend resources and energy to guess the random number in order to be rewarded with new Bitcoin. The nature of proof of work requires individual miners to compete using computer processing power to find the random number.

Without going into the technical depths of proof of work, the mechanism is designed to not only reward miners, but to protect the system by ensuring that attacks on the network are costly. A huge amount of computing power is needed in order to overtake or interrupt the network. The larger the Bitcoin network becomes in terms of miners, the more resources it requires to create a full network attack. Miners, who spend energy to mine Bitcoin, are incentivised through rewards to keep the network honest. At the same time, attackers are disincentivized to interfere with the protocol due to the number of resources and amount of energy required, making an attack infeasible. There is positive reinforcement, through the block reward, to ensure miners act honestly.

The combined computing power of the Bitcoin network is growing over time as more miners join the network. This can be seen by viewing the Bitcoin hash rate (Fig 1). The hash rate represents how many attempts at solving the math problem is carried out by the network and measured in 'exahashes'. There are quintillions of attempts to solve this math problem per second. As the network grows, the security increases, making it more expensive to attack Bitcoin.

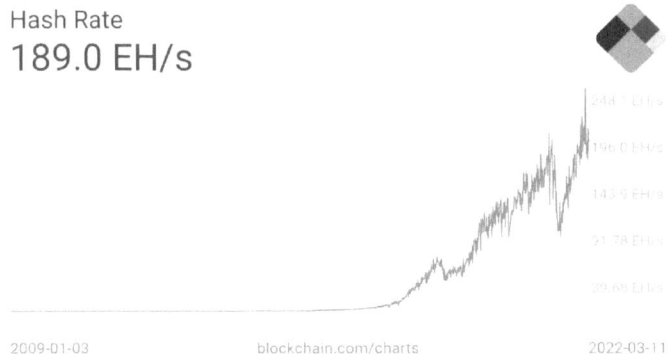

Fig 1 - *The Bitcoin Hash Rate 2009 to 2022 - The estimated number of exahashes per second the bitcoin network is performing*

The Bitcoin Halving and Supply

Now we know that Bitcoin was introduced in 2009 and there are 21 million Bitcoin. But how did Satoshi Nakamoto introduce the supply of Bitcoin to the public? And were all 21 million available to be bought or transferred on Day 1?

Satoshi Nakamoto designed the Bitcoin protocol to produce a certain amount of bitcoin roughly every 10 minutes using the proof of work mechanism. We know that proof of work is a system designed to use computing power to find a random number to get rewarded in Bitcoin and approve transactions. When Bitcoin was first introduced in 2009, 50 Bitcoin were released every 10 minutes to the network of miners.

There is an event called **the halving** that is built in to the protocol which occurs roughly every 4 years, or 210,000 blocks. This mechanism halves the number of Bitcoin the protocol releases. So, if the protocol released 50 Bitcoin every 10 minutes in the beginning, the next halving event halved the reward to 25 Bitcoin every 10 minutes.

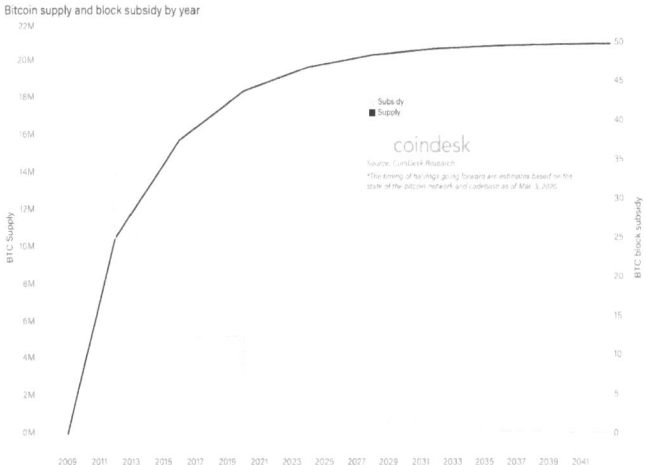

The Bitcoin Supply (Black Left) and Mining Reward (Yellow Right)

Here is a summary of Bitcoin halving and supply:

- There are 21 million Bitcoin in total

- New Bitcoin are produced roughly every 10 minutes

- Every 4 years, or 210,000 blocks, the supply of new Bitcoin is cut in half – e.g., 50 Bitcoin to 25 Bitcoin to 12.5 Bitcoin to 6.25 etc.

- The first halving took place on November 2012, the next on July 2016, and the third halving on May 2020. The next Halving will take place roughly April 2024.

- Over 90% of the Bitcoin supply, almost 19 million, is in circulation by the start of 2022

- The remaining 10% of supply will be released between 2022 and 2140 – almost 120 years!

The main reason for Satoshi Nakamoto introducing the halving was to allow the supply of Bitcoin to be controlled by the protocol and not by a central authority or institution. The halving means the rate of issuance to slow over time, making it more scarce, which may increase the demand for Bitcoin, increase the price, and lead to more adoption.

Halving Event	Date	Block Number	Reward per Block	Bitcoin Per Day
Bitcoin Launch	Jan 3rd 2009	0	50 Bitcoin	7200
First Halving	Nov 28th 2012	210,000	25 Bitcoin	3600
Second Halving	July 9th 2016	420,000	12.5 Bitcoin	1800
Third Halving	May 11th 2020	630,000	6.25 Bitcoin	900
Fourth Halving	Projected March 2024	840,000	3.125 Bitcoin	450
Fifth Halving	Projected May 2028	1,050,000	1.5625 Bitcoin	225

First 5 halving events in the Bitcoin protocol which reduces the supply over time

At the first ever halving event on November 28th 2012, the Bitcoin reward was cut in half, meaning only 25 bitcoins were released roughly every 10 minutes instead of 50 prior to the halving. The reduced supply means that those engaging as miners in the proof of work system are rewarded less – So, if miners are competing for these rewards using proof of work, does the halving of new supply lead to less desire on the side of the miners to obtain Bitcoin rewards?

With the issuing decreasing, the amount of new Bitcoin available to purchase also decreases. Based on scarcity in economics, scarce assets increase in value over time. Therefore, while the reward produced every 10 minutes has decreased, the value of Bitcoin should increase due to it becoming more scarce over time. This means, although those competing for the Bitcoin rewards receive less Bitcoin, the overall value of those Bitcoin rewards should increase.

Bitcoin has been a success for a number of reasons. Satoshi, having mined 1 million Bitcoin, should be one of the richest people on the planet but instead choose to walk away and leave Bitcoin the protocol in the hands of the community and the leave his/her mined Bitcoin untouched. This is an important ethical decision in the history of Bitcoin.

The way Bitcoin emerged, the incentives of the components of the protocol, the organic growth, and the disappearance of its creator are what makes Bitcoin unique and truly decentralized. This unusual set of circumstances is unlikely to repeat ever again.

Summary of Section 2 - What is Bitcoin and Why Bitcoin was Created.

In this section we asked the questions: what is Bitcoin and why was Bitcoin created? We Outlined what Bitcoin is. We looked at how Bitcoin is the most scarce asset that has ever existed. We learned that Bitcoin has 21 million Bitcoin and each Bitcoin can be fractionalized and transacted in Sats. We dove in to the incentives brought about by the proof of work mechanism and how miners are incentivised to protect the Bitcoin network by enforcing trust. We looked at how the Bitcoin protocol controls the supply and inflation of Bitcoin through the 4-year halving. Lastly, we garnered insights into the creator of Bitcoin, Satoshi Nakamoto, and Satoshi's intentions of allowing Bitcoin to organically grow, along with the importance of having a transparent, trusted system where no central government or authority is needed, eliminating the chance of influence and manipulation.

On your journey to understanding Bitcoin in its entirety, the next section will explore more on the technology and core components relating to the Bitcoin protocol. The section will help you understand how the technology works, along with why Satoshi introduced these ingenious components.

Why Bitcoin

Section 3

Bitcoin Technology

The Bitcoin Blockchain

The Bitcoin Blockchain is blocks of information chained together, one after another in chronological order. Bitcoin is essentially one giant list or ledger that keeps growing. The blockchain keeps track of all the transactions within the Bitcoin network. For example, Person A sent X Bitcoin to Person B, Person Z sent X Bitcoin to Person Y, and so on.

The blockchain keeps track of all transactions that have ever taken place on the Bitcoin network, right back to the very first block, the genesis block, created by Satoshi Nakamoto in 2009. One of the key aspects of the Bitcoin blockchain is that it is a **distributed ledger** - meaning the records of transactions, the ledger, is distributed widely among nodes (computers) all over the world.

The software to run a Bitcoin node can be downloaded to home computers and laptops. Once downloaded, individuals can run the software from their location. When a user downloads the software to run Bitcoin, they are also downloading the history of transactions on the ledger – The Bitcoin Blockchain.

The software allows you to be a node on the network. A Bitcoin node will automatically validate transactions by following the protocol rules, communicating with other nodes and ensuring the blockchain is harmonious. Each node has its own copy of the ledger which can validate the history of transactions by talking to other nodes in the network.

With individuals having the ability to download the software on home computers ensures the network is more decentralized as more people join the network and validate transactions.

If a record in the blockchain didn't add up, for example, if records show person A owned 2 Bitcoin but that person tried to create a false transaction that stated they had 4 Bitcoin, the network of nodes, which have the latest version of the ledger and talk to each other, would look back at the history of the ledger and reject this transaction for being invalid.

The nodes also contain the list of rules set out in the protocol, so if a node stated the number of Bitcoin exceeded the number set in the protocol (21 million), the transaction would also be rejected by all the other nodes in the network.

When nodes on the network agree that the transaction is valid based on the protocol rules, the transaction is batched with other valid transactions in a block. Proof of work is completed by the miners; the block is then 'glued' to the blockchain and communicated by the network of nodes and broadcast to the world.

A blockchain, or ledger, allows the network to maintain trust by having the nodes and miners on the network verify the history and integrity of the ledger, instead of a central authority.

Bitcoin Mining and the Difficulty Adjustment

Why Is Bitcoin Mining Important?

Bitcoin mining has 3 main function which we'll dive in to:

- Issuing new Bitcoin (according to the protocol schedule - covered in The Bitcoin Halving chapter)

- Securing the network from attacks

- Confirming transactions

Assets or money can be referred to as hard or easy, in relation to how hard or easy they are to produce. Bitcoin mining is similar to gold-mining, in the sense that it takes effort to mine the asset. Each piece of Gold above ground level is proof that work has been carried out, through machinery or human effort, to extract gold from the earth.

Fiat money, on the other hand, is very effortless and easy to produce. Central governments can simply increase the supply quickly and without effort, given that there is no hard asset backing the currency. Using this logic, Bitcoin and Gold are harder money than Fiat. Is it concerning that today's money can be inflated very easily by central authorities - What are the consequences for society when this new system, created in 1971, allows monetary units to be created with ease?

Bitcoin mining is not only a method for issuing new Bitcoin, which we covered, but also a mechanism that protects and secures the network.

Ensuring that someone must spend energy to obtain Bitcoin, ensures that attempts to create fraudulent transactions on the network are essentially wasted energy. A fraudulent attempt would costs the user time, resources and energy, as the nodes would reject any blocks that contain invalid data – remember, nodes are validating the entire history of the blockchain, so they can easily detect an invalid transaction. Does it make sense to attempt to spend resources creating a fraudulent action on the network, just for it to be rejected? If someone with an abundant, cheap energy source had the choice to attack the network and fail, or join the network and collect rewards, if that person was rational, they would join the network and collect the rewards instead of risking a failed, extremely costly, attempt at an attack.

With Bitcoin producing a block every 10 minutes, the more time that passes, the more transaction records get written to the chain, the longer the chain gets. The longer the chain is, the more difficult it is to change its history. This leads to an increase in network security. In order to change the history of transactions, you would need to spend a huge amount of money and resources to rewrite the existing chain of blocks. As the chain expands and the network of miners grow, it becomes costlier to attempt a fraudulent act. In a sense, Bitcoin is becoming more secure every 10 minutes as more blocks are created and even more secure as more miners join the network.

As mentioned previously, miners get rewarded for validating new blocks every 10 minutes. They also get a fee from users of the network when a transaction is created. When miners mine a block and confirm transactions, they are rewarded with an amount of Bitcoin. The reward is a positive feedback mechanism for the miner to keep the network secure. If you were a miner and dependent on the mining and transaction rewards as income, wouldn't you ensure the network remains secure and decentralized, where no individual or group of individuals can interfere?

What if you simply added more miners to the network, wouldn't that mean blocks are created quicker than the 10 minutes expected? A beautiful feature built into Bitcoin is the **difficulty adjustment**. As more miners enter the system, the Bitcoin protocol will automatically increase the difficulty of creating new blocks. Similarly, if miners leave the network, the protocol will decrease the difficulty of creating new blocks. That way the Bitcoin network ensures the average time to create new blocks remains at 10 minutes. The difficult adjustment feature in the protocol acts like a suspension system, ensuing the network always reverts back to 10-minute block times. This feature is unique when comparing it to the supply of other assets. It means that adding more resources does not equate to more supply of the asset.

As a simple example, in 2022, roughly 900 Bitcoin are released each day to miners. In a hypothetical example, if 900 miners existed and all had the same computing power, each miner could get 1 Bitcoin in mining rewards per day. If another 900 miners decided to join the network with the same computing resources – does this mean:

a. 1800 Bitcoin are rewarded to the 1800 miners

b. 900 Bitcoin are rewarded to the 1800 miners

The answer is B - Bitcoin will still only produce 900 Bitcoin per day, so the 1800 miners would be rewarded with 0.5 Bitcoin each and not 1 Bitcoin each.

In Bitcoin, if you try to force the supply, the protocol will rebalance, based on the resources on the network, to return to 10-minute block rewards. In other assets, like gold, we used the same theory - if 900 gold miners produced 900 ounces of gold per day and 900 extra gold miners joined the gold mining industry - it would be possible that 1800 ounces of gold could be produced daily, increasing the supply. It is also possible to engineer better, more efficient gold mining equipment and thereby increase the supply of gold.

With Bitcoin, the rules of the protocol govern the supply. In other assets, adding more resources or more powerful tools can increase the supply. In Bitcoin, the supply cannot be controlled or forced by adding more resources to the network or by creating more efficient tools.

The difficulty adjustment and Bitcoin's open-source nature ensures the Bitcoin supply is consistent, stable, and transparent.

The Bitcoin Network of Nodes

The Importance of Bitcoin Nodes

We have looked at the Bitcoin Network of Nodes in the Bitcoin Blockchain chapter, but let's dive in to more details on this. The Bitcoin nodes are computers connected to each other, following the rules of the Bitcoin protocol and sharing information between each node. The nodes, by consensus, validate transactions before they are added to the Bitcoin Blockchain. We also know that having nodes placed all over the world ensures one central party doesn't have control over the rules and validation of transactions.

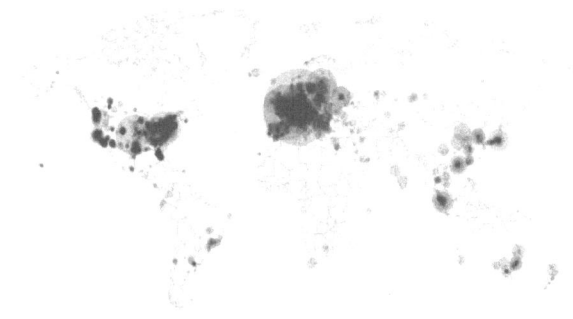

Graphic showing global distribution of Bitcoin Nodes from Bitnode.io

As mentioned before, nodes can be set up to run on home computers and laptops by downloading the software and the history of the blockchain. Satoshi understood that in order to keep the software in the control of the people, the blockchain couldn't grow so large in size that personal computers could not download the Bitcoin ledger.

The key to keeping the Bitcoin ledger small is to keep the size of each block added every 10 minutes small. Each block is storing bits of data. By having the minimum amount of data in each block, it ensures that many years from now the Bitcoin ledger size will stay within the rate of technology growth for personal computers. In 2022, anywhere from 250GB to 2 TB hard drive is standard for home computers. At the beginning of 2022 the total size of the Bitcoin Blockchain is ~380GB. Satoshi calculated that with technology efficiencies in the future and having a small, limited block size, the Bitcoin blockchain and nodes can be downloaded by home computers today and in the future.

From the Bitcoin Whitepaper Written by Satoshi Nakamoto:

A block header with no transactions would be about 80 bytes. If we suppose blocks are generated every 10 minutes, 80 bytes

* 6 * 24 * 365 = 4.2MB per year. With computer systems typically selling with 2GB of RAM as of 2008, and Moore's Law predicting current growth of 1.2GB per year, storage should not be a problem even if the block headers must be kept in memory.

Again, having the ledger size limited in size allows standard computers to run a node, which means more participation by users, which ensuring Bitcoin is widespread and remains decentralized. Currently the block size is 1MB per block. If the Bitcoin block size was to be increased to 10MB as an example, which has been attempted before, it would mean the Bitcoin ledger would grow 10 times in size in the same amount of time. Eventually and rather quickly, only large data centres would be able to run the Bitcoin software. Personal computers would no longer be suitable for running The Bitcoin node software. This could leave Bitcoin vulnerable to centralized control for those companies or organizations that owned big data centers – we're looking at you Amazon, Google, and Microsoft.

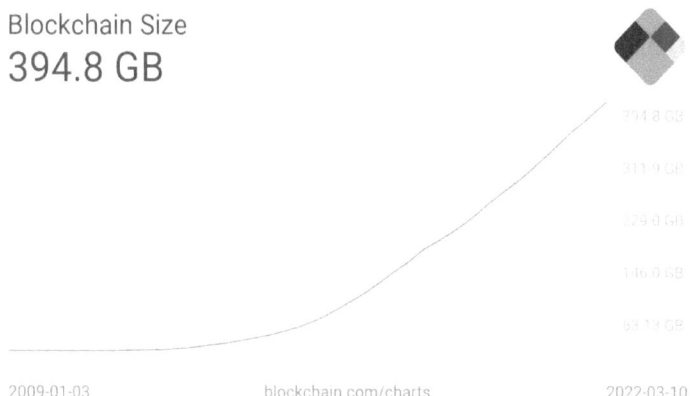

Bitcoin Blockchain size Jan 2009 to March 2022 from blockchain.com

A key feature of Bitcoin is the ability for everyone to run a node to validate transactions, from a personal computer, ensuring Bitcoin stays decentralized.

Bitcoin Consensus

Can Bitcoin Be Changed by Anyone?

As aforementioned, Bitcoin is an open-source protocol. Bitcoin is code. Bitcoin has rules. For example, the rules state there will be 21 million Bitcoin within the protocol.

What if a user wanted to make a change to the rules of Bitcoin? What if someone wanted to double the number of Bitcoin to, say, 42 million Bitcoin? Is it possible and, if so, how would someone go about doing this?

The Bitcoin protocol has been upgraded in the past through proposals by the community. Bitcoin has also been forked in the past. A fork is when another version of Bitcoin code is introduced which splits from the core protocol; users can choose to follow and use another protocol if they want or to remain on the current version of Bitcoin. In the past following another protocol has been proven to a poor decision for the proposers of the fork, as the community has always remained on the main Bitcoin protocol.

A Bitcoin Improvement Proposal (BIP) can be drafted by anyone but having the proposal introduced to the system isn't an easy task by any means. The process of introducing a new BIP is not as straight forward as a yes/no approval. It requires 95% agreement from the community. With the potential of economic loss at stake, every decision is scrutinized by users in order to protect the Bitcoin ecosystem.

As an example, we can hypothetically create our own Bitcoin client and we can start a marketing campaign to get people to run our version of Bitcoin. It may go something like this:

> Us: *'Hi, we wrote a Bitcoin client that rewards us with 1% of all transactions, we've released it, would you run it for us?'*
>
> The community and any sane individual: *'No'*
>
> It really is that simple, the user chooses which software to run.

We have seen in previous chapters how the components of Bitcoin are designed with incentives to protect and secure the network. The rules of Bitcoin are also protected by the users by incentivising good behavior. The users of the network spend resources and energy to protect the network, while also holding an asset that is valuable to them. This means that it is in the interest of the users to ensure that any proposal to change the rules are for the betterment of Bitcoin. Satoshi understood that upgrading the Bitcoin protocol would be necessary over time, but also understood that those who have something to lose should be the people deciding if a proposal should be introduced or not.

In Bitcoin, it is the miners/nodes all over the world who secure the network and get rewarded for confirming transactions. If you are a miner, you'll be running a node to ensure transactions and rewards are valid. If a bad upgrade was introduced, the miners and holders of Bitcoin could suffer economic loss. Accounting for this, it makes sense that the miner/nodes are the ones who decide if a proposal gets approved or not.

This consensus mechanism ensures that any proposal for rule changes is beneficial to the ecosystem, does not put the ecosystem at risk and, most importantly, ensures Bitcoin is immune to central authority decision making.

Wallets and Addresses

How Can I Transact and Store Bitcoin?

Since the introduction of computers and the internet, many of our physical assets have moved from physical form to digital form. Take, for example, music. In previous times, music has been distributed and transported in a physical manner through vinyl records and CDs. Since the introduction of computers, music can be accessed from hard drives. Furthermore, since the introduction of the internet, music can now be accessed from the cloud.

Books, movies, and photographs have followed the same transition from physical to digital access. Bitcoin, being a digital asset, can also be accessed on computers and the internet.

Having access to Bitcoin requires you to have a digital wallet. Before we look at Bitcoin wallets, we must first have a general understanding of how Bitcoin is moved from one place to another. There are 3 key components to understanding the spending, withdrawal, and transfer of

Bitcoin. There are **Bitcoin addresses, private keys, and Bitcoin wallets.**

Think of **Bitcoin addresses** as the place where users go to send or receive Bitcoin. Think of your Bitcoin address much like an email address. Just like email address, your Bitcoin address is your public address which can be given to people if you want to receive Bitcoin.

Private keys are what give a user access to the Bitcoin at their address. The private key, often referred to as your digital signature, is a secret number that is used to protect your Bitcoin and give access to your Bitcoin. Private Keys are generated and protected by cryptography. This makes private keys the most important and robust component of your personal Bitcoin security. If a user loses their private key, they will no longer have access to Bitcoin at that address and can no longer spend, withdraw, or transfer the Bitcoin from their address.

Bitcoin wallets are used to store your keys. It is important to understand that a wallet doesn't store your bitcoin, it only stores your private keys to access your Bitcoin. Your Bitcoin will always remain on the blockchain. The wallet can be used to sign transactions using your private key if you want to transact in Bitcoin.

Now that we understand that:

- A Bitcoin address is where you send or receive Bitcoin
- A private key is used to access your Bitcoin
- And a wallet is used to store your private keys required for transactions

Let's look at how to spend, withdraw, and transfer Bitcoin.

To spend, withdraw, or transfer Bitcoin, you need to access your wallet, you need to know the Bitcoin address you are sending the bitcoin to, and you need to digitally sign the transaction using your private key. This can all be done within a Bitcoin wallet.

To receive Bitcoin, you need to provide the sender your public address and the sender should follow the steps listed previously to send you Bitcoin.

Even though this process may sound simple in some ways and complicated in other ways, many of the send-and-receive steps are being simplified using software to create better user experiences and interfaces, including sending and receiving Bitcoin from wallets easily using QR codes.

Now we understand how Bitcoin can be transacted and that private keys are the most important component of Bitcoin security, what are the options for storing your private keys on wallets?

Private keys can be stored in 2 ways. Either on self-custody wallets by the user or in custodial wallets handled by a third party on the user's behalf.

An example of a self-custody wallet is a hardware wallet. A USB drive that you store in a secure location. This option gives you full control over your private keys.

Hardware wallets keep your private keys stored offline, often referred to as cold storage, adding a layer of security from any potential online hacks. As part of the hardware wallet, you will also have a recovery phrase in case you lose or damage your hardware wallet. You can generate your own recovery phrase but most hardware wallets generate a recovery phrase for you. If you cannot access your hardware wallet for any reason, you can simply purchase a new hardware wallet, enter the recovery phrase, and gain access to your private keys again. Technically, if you choose to memorise your recovery phrase, you can travel anywhere in the world with your private keys stored in your head. This protects your Bitcoin from any confiscation and allows you to move your Bitcoin in a borderless manner and access your Bitcoin anywhere in the world. Having a hardware wallet and a recovery phrase prevents authorities from confiscating your Bitcoin.

Another version of a self-custody wallets is to use a software wallet. This type of wallet is an application on your mobile or desktop which is connected to the internet. Software wallets also come with a recovery phrase.

Although software wallets have reached a high level of security during the past few years, there is still a risk of being hacked due to it being connected to the internet.

The other option to store private keys is to choose a custodial service to hold your private keys for you. It is important that you understand who is handling your private keys if you choose this option. You are handing your Bitcoin keys to a third party, so trust is of the upmost importance. Some custodial services choose to hold your Bitcoin in their wallets, rather than holding your private keys. If you transfer your Bitcoin to a custodian service, it is much like an IOU. The number of custodial services for Bitcoin is increasing every year and the custodial services are improving security processes over time. This option may be helpful for those who have trust in a third party holding your private keys.

Having multiple options to store your private keys is good for users of Bitcoin and will increase adoption. Doing your own research to understand the security and risks of storing, accessing, and confiscation of your private keys is important when making your decision.

Summary of Section 3

In this section, we looked at the technical components of Bitcoin in more detail. We looked at the Blockchain and how it keeps a secure, distributed record of all transactions all over the world. We explored the process of introducing new Bitcoin in to the system through Bitcoin mining. We looked at how newly introduced Bitcoin are first validated by the vast network of nodes, ensuring no fraudulent activity takes place on the blockchain. We looked at how the community controls the future of Bitcoin through consensus, ensuring the ecosystem functions in the best interest of the users. And finally, we looked at how Bitcoin wallets and address's function to store and transact in Bitcoin.

Section 4

The Emergence of Bitcoin

Analogue to Digital

In the previous 2 sections we covered what Bitcoin is and why it was created. This section is an added bonus section to explain the emergence of Bitcoin as an asset in today's world and to discuss where Bitcoin is potentially headed in the future.

There are many examples in recent history of technological advancements replacing manual, analogue solutions. Many of these transitions are obvious when looking back now, but at the time of introduction, adoption was not straight forward. Quite a lot of the struggle for technology adoption comes down to a few factors: Human behaviour, lack of education and/or parties who are benefitting from the current system and therefore refuse to move to a new system or technology. Many of the people opposing the new technology have large investment in the analogue version, which is threatened by a new technological solution.

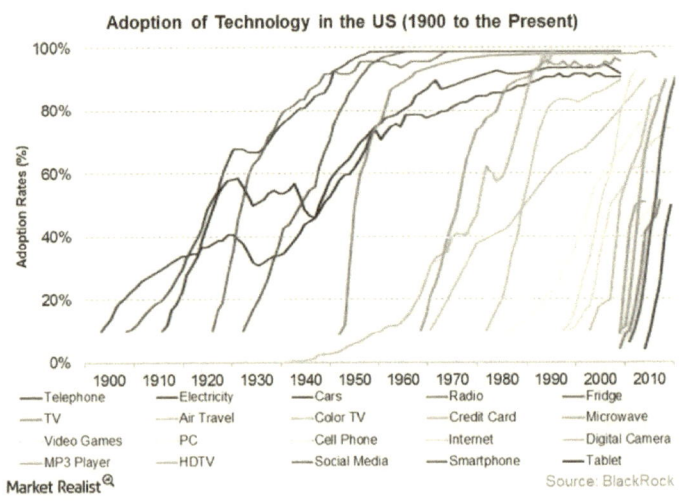

BlackRock on the adoption of Technology in the US from 1900 to 2015

Several studies have shown that technology adoption has increased at a faster rate in recent times. A study by BlackRock on the adoption of Technology in the US from 1900 to 2015 shows trends of technology adoption is increasing. For example, the telephone took almost 25 years to get to 40% adoption in the US from 1900 to 1925. For comparison, it took smart phones less than 3 years in the 2000's to reach 80% adoption in the US. This trend has been consistent by showing technologies such as Electricity, Cars, and Radio taking more than a decade in the early 1900's to reach 50% adoption. Since the 2000's, MP3 players, social media, and smart phones have taken less than 3 years to reach 50% adoption. Bitcoin is estimated to be at the early adaptors phase with less than 10% adoption in the US in 2021 and single figure percentages in terms of global adoption rates.

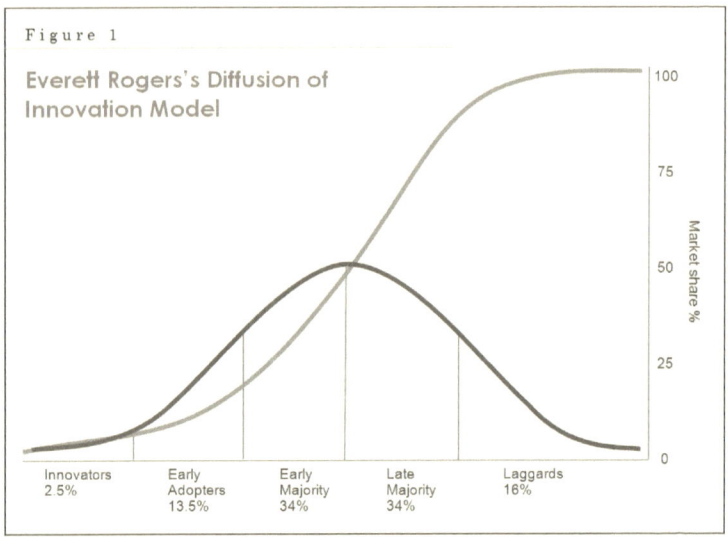

Figure 1

Everett Rogers's Diffusion of Innovation Model

Innovators 2.5%
Early Adopters 13.5%
Early Majority 34%
Late Majority 34%
Laggards 16%

Cars have been around for over a century. The automobile eventually replaced many of the task's horses performed. It is easy to see now why it was beneficial to replace horses with cars, but the transition was not a straightforward one. Many thought that horses couldn't be replaced by cars. Cars were deemed dangerous, unnecessary, and inconvenient at first. When cars were introduced, the infrastructure that we know today wasn't around – Roads didn't exist like we know them today. Fueling was very inconvenient and fueling stations were sparse. Did people instantly trust these huge chunks of metal driving around at high speeds? Certainly, there were opposers at the time, but humanity would be many decades behind if we stood in the way of the growth of the automotive ecosystem and industry.

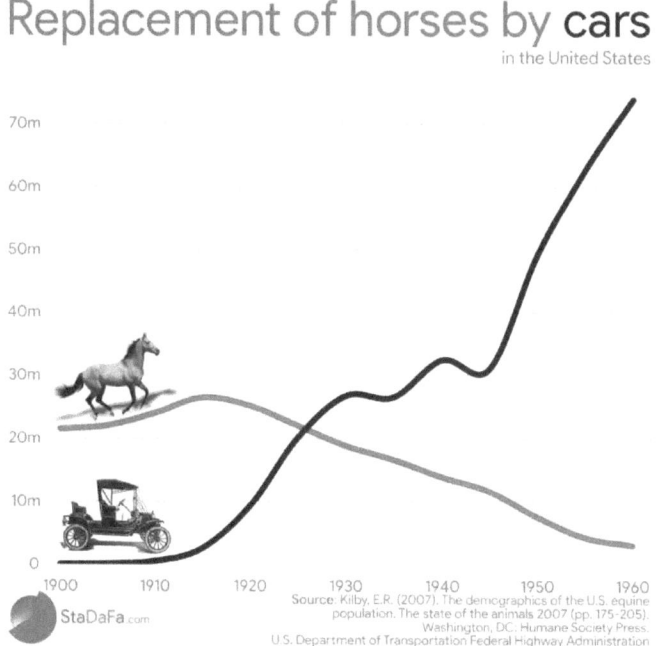

In recent times, many other technological advancements suffered similar push back and criticism from the industry that the technology threatened to replace. In December 2000, the Daily Mail, who were in the physical newspaper business, posted a headline in their newspaper which read – Internet

'May be just a passing fad as millions give up on it.'

Did newspaper companies want the internet to succeed? Would they have been more successful if they adopted the new technology and embrace the internet?

Did the businesses who benefitted from supplying horses and carriages want cars to succeed? Would they have been more successful if they adopted the new technology and embraced cars?

Does the fossil fuel industry want green energy to succeed? Would they be more successful if they adopted the new technology and embraced renewable energy solutions?

Based on previous and current adoption struggles, if we describe Bitcoin as being a trust-less peer-to-peer version of electronic cash, which required no trusted third-party, while also being a potential replacement for gold – Do you think traditional financial institutions and gold bugs would want Bitcoin to succeed? Would they be more successful if they adopted the new technology and embraced Bitcoin?

Gold is the analogue version of neutral money; Bitcoin is the digital version.

The current banking system, where humans control the inflation rate, is the analogue version. Bitcoin, with a programmatically set supply, is the digital version.

Based on history it may be best for industries to adopt new technologies and work it into their product and services rather than acting against it.

In modern times, the Internet is the technology that most similarly resembles Bitcoin in terms of a digital, nascent technology. The internet and the protocol TCP/IP were created in the 1970's and had some breakthroughs in the 1980's but it wasn't until the late 1990's, over 2 decades later, that saw the Internet reach mainstream adoption. In the 1980's and early 1990's the internet didn't seem obvious to most and originally faced pushback. Only in hindsight was it obvious this would be a technology to advance society. The following 2 decades (2000's and 2010's) saw the internet become ingrained into every part of society. Bitcoin, created in 2009, had some breakthroughs in the 2010's. Will the 2020's be the decade where it becomes mainstream, growing ever present in daily lives with adoption continuing the next few decades until mass adoption, just like the internet did?

Bitcoin vs Gold

How Does Bitcoin Compare to Gold?

We covered how gold was the best form of money for thousands of years and how it prevailed as money as it competed against other metals and succeeded due to its superior properties as money.

Many investors invest in gold to protect their purchasing power against the inflation of fiat currency, citing that gold's scarcity will result in an increase in value as the money supply of fiat increases much faster than gold's supply.

Let's compare Bitcoin and Gold with the same properties from earlier and add in some more attributes that are required based on the evolution of money from the early days.

	Bitcoin	Gold
Durable	B+	A
Portable	A	C
Divisible	A	C
Recognizable	B	B
Scarce	A	B
Verifiable	A	B
Censorship resistant	A	B
Cost of storage	A	C

Although Bitcoin is almost perfect when it comes to **durability**, it does rely on the internet and electricity to function. If the internet and electricity wasn't available, Bitcoin wouldn't function, but gold could, technically, be of use for local transactions. Although a global internet or electricity outage is a possibility, it is an extremely unlikely occurrence. This is the only property of money that gold has an advantage over Bitcoin and only in a particular set of circumstances.

An enormous advantage Bitcoin has over gold is **portability.** If you were to transfer $10,000 of gold from the US to Japan on the weekend, how easy would it be, taking in to consideration access, administration, shipping costs, and duration to transport the gold? If you were to transfer the same amount of Bitcoin from US to Japan at the weekend, how easy would it be? Bitcoin is a 24/7, 365-day, permissionless, borderless monetary network that can be settled almost instantly.

When we explored the flaws in gold, it was clear that Satoshi strived to eliminate these flaws as well as improve on the properties of Gold - let's take a look at Golds flaws and how Bitcoin improved upon them.

Confiscation – Gold has been previously confiscated by government. Bitcoin can be kept safe and offline, meaning authoritarians cannot take Bitcoin from users. Once you store your Bitcoin offline or have your recovery phrase in your head, it can be transported and stored with you at all times and out of reach of everyone else.

Improvements on Gold's Flaws

Portability – Gold is difficult and expensive to move across time and space. Bitcoin, however, can be transferred across the world almost instantly.

Scarcity – Gold isn't a fixed supply asset and more can be produced over time. No matter how much human energy and creativity you throw at Bitcoin, you cannot force more Bitcoin from the system – there will only be 21 million Bitcoin. Bitcoin's supply and supply schedule is set in stone.

Verifiability – It is not known how much gold there is in the world. Bitcoin, on the other hand, is built on open-source code on a blockchain. Anyone can verify the rules, the supply, the distribution of Bitcoin, how many Bitcoin have been mined to date, how many Bitcoin are mined per day, how many wallets hold Bitcoin and much more. This data is all available on the public Bitcoin blockchain.

Divisibility – Gold can be divisible but only by using specific tools. 1 Bitcoin can be divided in to 100 million pieces (Satoshi's) without the need for specialist equipment.

Other Improvements

Storage – The more gold you buy, the more storage space you require. If you store gold in a vault, there will be a storage cost. With Bitcoin, storage space is not an issue. Whether you buy 10 thousand Satoshi's or 10 million Satoshi's, storage space, it is the same.

Gold can be of use in the 21st century if you put it in a bag and use it as a weapon, but if you compare Gold's money properties and flaws to a digital asset like Bitcoin, Satoshi Nakamoto has successfully and significantly improved upon the properties of money.

Bitcoin Vs Fiat

How Does Bitcoin Compare to Fiat Money?

As mentioned previously, fiat money is money issued by order, by a government, and controlled by a central authority or central bank.

One of the more easily relatable versions of fiat money is the US dollar. With the US dollar being the global reserve currency, we will focus on the US fiat and dollar system, which is controlled by the US central bank, the Federal Reserve. The principles in this section can be applied to any fiat system.

Since US President Nixon decoupled money from gold in 1971, the dollar and other currencies haven't been backed by a hard to produce asset. This means that the future inflation rate of the dollar is unknown. Again, Bitcoin has a supply of 21 million which doesn't inflate. The dollar, because it is controlled by a central authority, can have an unlimited supply if a central authority decides. To date, the supply of dollars has only increased over the long term and at an accelerated rate.

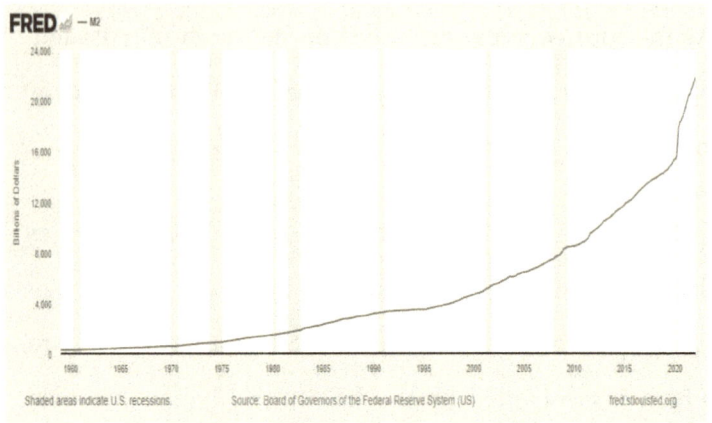

M2 Money supply in the US 1950's to 2022 - https://fred.stlouisfed.org/series/M2SL

When it comes to the properties of money, we know that Bitcoin is a superior version of money, when compared with gold. Bitcoin is based on the properties of money, but it is also an improvement on these properties, where its predecessor gold was used for thousands of years as a monetary system. Even though Bitcoin does not have a long track record, it is still based on the economics of hard asset properties, like gold, which has been in place for thousands of years. Fiat, on the other hand, has been in place for less than 6 decades. In a way you could say that the fiat system is still an experiment given that the world had never fully operated in this type of monetary system, prior to its recent introduction.

Inflation is a term mainly used in economics but is understood fundamentally by everyone. As an example, if you had $10 in 1990 you could buy more than 20 cans of coca cola – 50c per can. Today the same $10 would get you less than 10 cans of coca cola – over $1 per can. Using this example, we can see that the same amount of dollars is purchasing less of the same good as time passes. This is referred to as **a loss of purchasing power**. The supply of the dollar has increased greatly since 1971. As mentioned previously, if more money supply is introduced in to the system, there will be more money chasing the same goods, resulting in inflation. Inflation leads to less purchasing power over time.

Why Bitcoin

Fixed assets like gold increased greatly following the introduction of fiat allowing governments to print unlimited money - researchgate.net

What if you worked hard to save $1000 or $10,000 and wanted to keep your money safe as cash or in a checking account for 30 years? Based on the historic purchasing power of the dollar, your $1000 or $10,000 would be significantly devalued through the printing of new currency, by those that control the money supply. Do you think people should be able to save their hard-earned money and keep it for future use without having to worry about losing purchasing power? The current fiat system doesn't allow for this to happen, as central issuers of the currency keep creating more and more units.

The price of McDonalds menu 1972 – Have McDonalds increased the quality of their food to justify price increases, or have prices simply increased due to the inflation of the money supply.

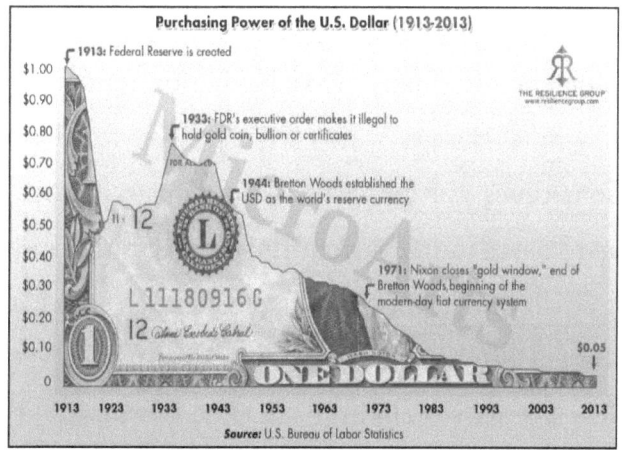

How the US dollar is losing purchasing power over time 1913 to 2013

Bitcoin has only been around since 2009 so it only has a short history, so far. However, in its short history, Bitcoin has appreciated immensely against fiat currencies. In economics, we know that scarcity increases value and abundance of supply decreases value. The fiat system, measured against a scarce asset like Bitcoin, is an example of scarcity leading to an increase in value against abundant assets. Over time there are more dollar units chasing the same amount of Bitcoin.

Many countries around the world have controls in place when it comes to currency. There are many third-world countries where a large part of the population doesn't have access to a banking system. Barriers to entry for the poor is a problem with many banks having minimum deposit limits, annual charges which are expensive for the poor, and sometimes upfront costs to participate. Quite often there are perks in the current financial system which are based on an individual's wealth. The rich often get access to different products and services, which the lower and middle classes are excluded from. The Fiat system is also built on currency borders where it is expensive to transfer and convert money from one country to another if the currency is different– e.g., transferring US dollars to Pesos can often be difficult and expensive, particularly for the poorest in society as some services operate on a flat fee basis, which is more substantial for those transferring small amounts of money. The fiat system is not an inclusive financial system that allows the transfer of money across borders with ease.

Technically you can use Bitcoin if you have a $50 android phone and an internet connection. There is no minimum deposit requirement or annual charges for participation in the Bitcoin system. Bitcoin is an all-inclusive monetary network that is borderless and permissionless. Bitcoin doesn't care what your background is, what your religion is, what your nationality is, what your sex is, if you are rich or poor, all holders of Bitcoin are treated the same - Bitcoin is neutral money.

The Bitcoin Price

I intentionally keep any discussion about the price of Bitcoin to the end of the journey. The price of Bitcoin is what draws a lot of people in, but it is important to first understand money, to understand why Bitcoin was created, and to understand the technology behind Bitcoin before looking at the price.

Bitcoin has been the best performing asset of the last decade out of all the asset classes, and by quite a margin – it has outperformed stocks, bonds, real estate, commodities (including gold) and cash. However, Bitcoin is a very new asset class in comparison to other asset classes. Depending on your time frame for investing, the results of investing can be positive or negative. In the short-term, Bitcoin can be volatile, but in the long term it continues to be the best performing asset. As with all new asset classes, volatility is normal in the early years. Luckily for Bitcoin investors, the long-term volatility is heavily on the upside. In 2021 Bitcoin reached a 1 trillion market cap for the first time. Bitcoin is the fastest asset to ever reach a

1 trillion-dollar market cap, beating gold, apple, google, Microsoft, and Amazon by decades.

Based on what we have discovered so far, Bitcoin's price increase can be attributed to 3 important factors, with one Bitcoin feature underpinning these factors. The factors are Inflation, The Halving, and the Adoption rate.

1. **Inflation** – We understand that the money supply of Fiat is controlled by a central authority. Over time the total number of dollars has increased over the long- term leading to inflation of goods, services, and assets.

The introduction of additional money in to the economy pushes prices up as there is a greater supply of money chasing the same goods. After the financial crisis in 2008/2009, more money was created using debt to help 'stimulate' the economy. This is often referred to as quantitative easing or simply as money printing. This worked in the short term. In the long term, the additional money created higher prices for goods, services and especially assets. This meant that people had to spend more money to get the same goods, reducing the purchasing power of savers. It also meant that wages needed to increase in line with the inflation of goods and services otherwise workers are doing the same work for less purchasing power.

The money supply continued to increase after 2008 and more aggressively in recent years. With more money in the economy, asset holders were the main beneficiary. Real estate, stocks (In particular tech stocks), and Bitcoin increased more rapidly. A quick google search for 'M2 money supply' will show you the increase in money supply going back decades. Bitcoin being a fixed asset means that more money is able to find its way towards the 21 million fixed supply.

2. **The Halving** – if you look at the price of Bitcoin, it increases in cycles. There is a lot of volatility over time but the general trend is skewed hugely to the upside. The restriction of the newly issued supply seems to create a price increase. The new supply of

Bitcoin will continue to half every 4 years until around 2140. If the supply of Bitcoin is going to slow in the long term and fiat money increasing in the long term, wouldn't the price of Bitcoin continue to increase against fiat currencies? We cannot rely on past performance as an indicator of future performance; however, in economics, supply and demand control the price of goods. Bitcoin and Fiat supply are going in opposite directions over time.

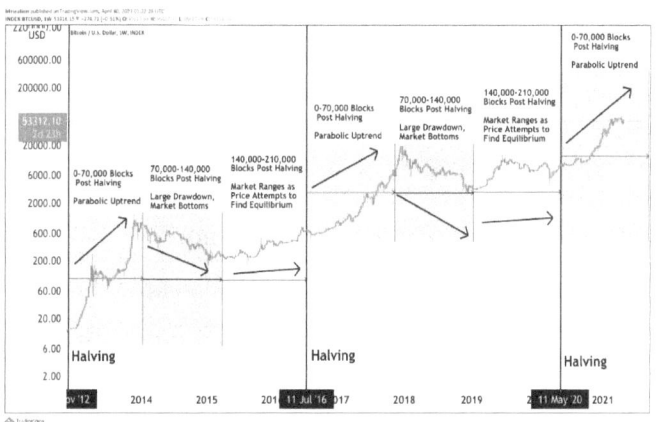

The Bitcoin Halving reduces the new supply which, to date, has resulted in huge increases in the Bitcoin Price -
https://www.zenledger.io/blog/bitcoin-halving-dates

When Amazon first went public, the stock price was very volatile. Some of the downward price movement was in excess of 50% on multiple occasions. This was most evident in the first 13 years of Amazon being a publicly traded company.

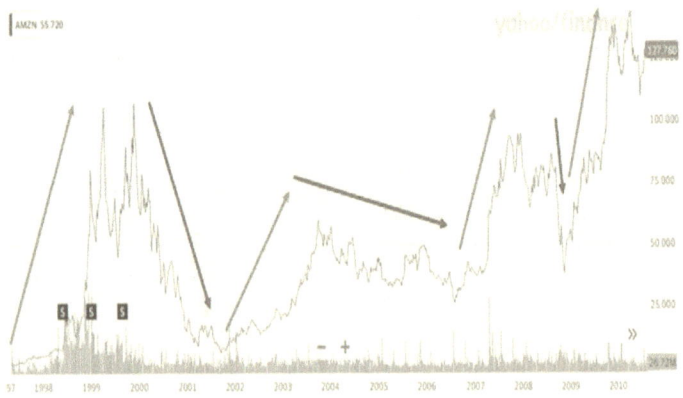

Amazon volatile share price the first 13 years of public trading – Yahoo finance

Most people failed to understand the impact of ecommerce in the early days of Amazon. As people started to understand the impact of the internet and online retail, Amazon's volatility reduced and Amazon's stock price increased to the upside significantly, becoming one of the best investments of the last few decades. Bitcoins first 13 year is comparable to Amazons first 13 years, with high volatility and a lack of general understanding by many people.

Amazon's volatility is negligible over the long term once the impact of online retail is realized. Investors were rewarded and those who invested during Amazon's most volatile years were heavily rewarded.

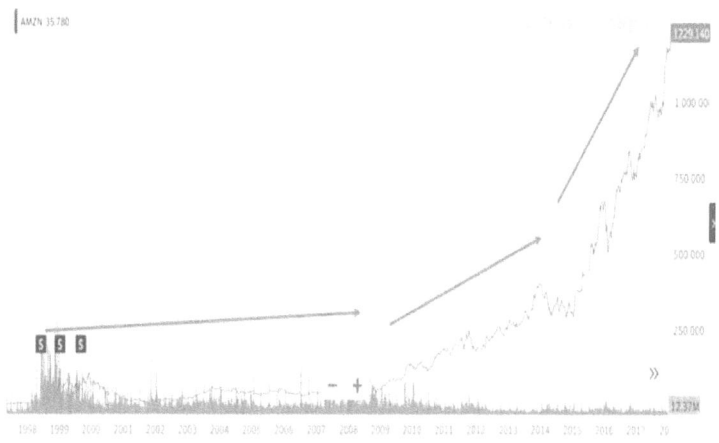

Amazon's long term share price 1997 to 2021 – Yahoo Finance

Bitcoin has historically reacted to the halving event and supply cut which has caused a lot of volatility. As time goes on and adoption grows, the reaction to the halving event could lessen. Volatility could be reduced as more people understand the true scarcity and potential of Bitcoin.

3. . Adoption Rate

We looked at how adoption of new technologies has been faster in recent decades. There are many reasons for this and one of them is the availability of information, thanks to the growth of the internet. We have also looked at how technology, in particular a digital version of a technology, has been successfully adopted historically. With Bitcoin being a digital version of money built on the internet, could it follow the recent technology adoption trends?

Every generation has the capability and ability to understand new technology. However, each generation has had a different level of exposure to technology and technology types, depending on which era someone was born into. The baby boomer generation, for example, are not native internet users, but they do hold the biggest portion of wealth of out of all current generations. In contrast, the millennial generation are native internet users but have the least wealth out of all generations from those generations who are able to participate (At the time of writing, only a portion of the Gen Z generation have reached the legal age to hold investments, and although Gen Z are extremely important for the future of Bitcoin, the generation are not included in this context). The millennial generation grew up in a different environment where the internet was commonplace in most households from when they were young. Digital versions of products are second-nature to the vast majority of millennials.

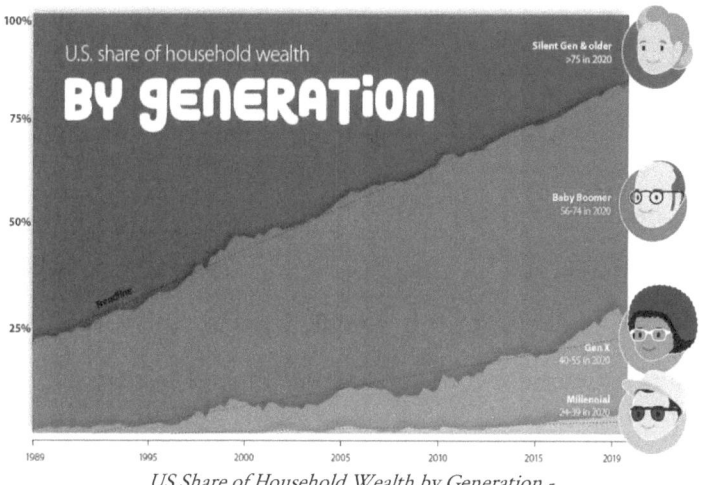

US Share of Household Wealth by Generation - https://www.visualcapitalist.com/charting-the-growing-generational-wealth-gap/

The use of libraries, physical maps, and CD's have been replaced with E-books/Audio Books, Google Maps, and iTunes/Spotify.

Bitcoin can often be referred to as a 'mirage', 'not real', 'magic internet money' by some of the older generations who haven't had the same exposure to digital products as younger generations had. If we look at the younger generations, many people understand the value of digital currencies from an early age. There are computer games in recent years that contain their own currency which users have exposure to at a young age and understand the concept of digital assets as a result. Fortnite, for example, has a currency called v-bucks that can be bought using fiat currency and exchanged for in-game items.

As the Millennials and Gen Z generation take up a more prominent role in the workforce and as more baby boomers move in to retirement, we will see more of the younger generation assume important roles in society in education, politics, and business. This could improve the adoption rate of Bitcoin – will the next group of CEOs of the major tech companies understand the potential of Bitcoin better than previous generations who are non-native internet users? Will a future presidential candidate or perhaps the winner of a presidential election understand the potential of Bitcoin better than the current people in power?

Inheritance is another factor in adoption. As wealth and assets are passed through generations, will the younger generation adopt a digit version rather than physical or analogue version of assets – if a millennial was passed some gold bars as inheritance from their parents, would they want to keep the gold bars and pay for storage while potentially seeing the demand for gold decrease. Or would a millennial want to sell part/all of the gold, buy Bitcoin, store it on their software or hardware wallet with no storage costs, and potentially see the adoption and demand for Bitcoin increase? According to data from Visual Capitalist in 2020, it is estimated that millennials will inherit over $68 trillion from baby boomer parents by 2030.

The 3 factors that drive Bitcoin's price – **inflation** due to fiat money supply, the **halving** reducing the new Bitcoin supply, and the **adoption** rate are all underpinned by one key attribute of Bitcoin – **Decentralization**.

Decentralization enables the rules of Bitcoin to remain consistent and in the best interest of the users over decades and even centuries. The fixed supply and its schedule are set in stone. Bitcoin is predictable, continuing to validate blocks every 10 minutes without failure, and is without human interference. Satoshi referenced **Trust** as a weakness in the financial system. Bitcoin fundamentals are based on **Trust**.

Bitcoin Total Addressable Market (TAM)

Does Bitcoin Have More Room to Grow?

The Total addressable market is the total market size available for a product if it achieved 100% market share.

For Example, the auto industry attracts a certain amount of value globally – let's say it's $10 Trillion today. This is the total allocation of capital that is held in the auto industry. Auto manufacturers compete for their share of the market. If for example, Tesla, occupied 20% of the auto industry market and Toyota occupied 10% of the market, then Tesla would be $2 trillion and Toyota would be value at $1 Trillion. Tesla and Toyota then have the opportunity to increase its market share to $10 Trillion but this means occupying 100% of the market share and wiping out the competition. This is extremely unlikely, especially in the services industry but in other areas, if you have the dominant use case with the ultimate product. Google, for example, has consistently retained over 80% market share in the search engine industry.

Bitcoin. However, isn't competing in the services industry, Bitcoin is competing on a much larger scale. Bitcoin is competing for the entire global asset market, which we'll dive into next.

First, we need to understand Bitcoins' current value and the size of the Market it is competing in.

The Market Cap of an asset tells you the current market value of an asset and is worked out using a simple calculation. It is calculated by multiplying the number of shares or units by the price of each unit. For example – if 1 Bitcoin was worth $100,000 and there were 21 million Bitcoin, the Market cap equates to $2.1 trillion. If apple shares are worth $100 each and Apple issued 1 billion shares, Apple's market cap would equate to $100 billion.

I will outline market cap figures based on present day values – 2022.

Today, Bitcoins' current Market cap which is, at the beginning of 2022, close to $1 trillion. Gold's Market cap at the same time is around $10 trillion. Given that Bitcoin has superior properties to gold, would it be fair to think that in the future the Bitcoin market cap could exceed gold's market cap? If Bitcoin equaled Gold's market cap of $10 trillion, each Bitcoin would be worth over $500,000. Bitcoin is not only an asset that is comparable to gold, but Bitcoin also has other use cases and advantages over some other assets. Can Bitcoin take the market share of other assets, further increasing the value of Bitcoin?

Keep in mind that the Bitcoin market cap is less than a $1 trillion asset by 2022 and has returned well in excess of 100% returns annually over the last decade.

Also remember that Bitcoin is an inclusive global monetary network that is borderless and permissionless, which gives Bitcoin even more value. As an example of a limitation of other assets, some stocks and bonds are only traded within a certain country or region. How easy is it to buy or sell real estate in a country on the other side of the world? These asset trading limitations can often make Bitcoin look like a more attractive investment.

Let's look at more examples of assets that exist today.

Bonds – Bonds are a steady investment for those looking for fixed income. However, bonds are only of use as an investment if the current inflation rate is less than the return of the bonds. If bonds are returning 2% per year it means a $1000 investment returns $20 on your initial investment. However, if the inflation rate is 4% then your purchasing power of the $1000 is worth $960 at the end of the year. This investment would have made you $20 but lost $40 in purchasing power resulting in a net loss of $20. Many Bonds are negative-yielding, meaning the return is less than inflation rate. This may change but currently bonds are losing money against current inflation rates.

The global bond market is estimated in **excess of a $100 trillion** market cap – could some of the money allocated to the bond market make its way to Bitcoin?

Real Estate – Real estate is purchased for 2 main reasons:

- For its utility, as shelter and a place to live.

- As an investment

Investors often purchase real estate as a store of value. Investors of property expect the value of the property to hold value over time, as it is a *hard to create* asset in relation to other assets. Real estate has been a safe and profitable investment against fiat currency historically. However, real estate usually comes with some one-off costs such as property taxes as well as maintenance and repairs. Buying and selling property also comes with administrative costs which are also time consuming. Currently selling property is not an easy process. It is not the most liquid market compared to other markets, by that I mean you cannot sell the asset today and expect settlement of funds today, tomorrow or even weeks. It can take months and often years to sell a property. As a result of not having the ability to sell a property as a fraction, selling property becomes much more difficult than selling other assets which can be fractionalised.

Property isn't the easiest asset to create, although with technological advances, such as 3D printing and advanced machinery, will it be easier than ever to create new property in the coming decade? Technological advancements in could increase the supply of property. Increased supply can lead to decreased scarcity and value.

Of course, real estate does have value by providing shelter and people will always pay for that, but is real estate also being used as a store of value **in the absence of a better store of value**. How much of real estate prices are set by the demand for shelter vs the demand as a store of value. If there was a better store of value asset known to all, would housing lose some of its value and be priced for its shelter utility, minus the store of value premium? Could this bring down housing prices and make housing affordable to those using housing for its utility only, a home, rather than a store of value asset also?

The global real estate market is estimated in **excess of a $200 trillion** market cap – could some of the money allocated to the real estate market make its way to Bitcoin?

Stocks – Stocks have been a great long-term investment in the last 2 centuries. Stocks rely on central figures to make good decisions for a company in order to produce goods and services that are desired. This in turn creates value and generates revenue and profits. Stocks can, and have been, diluted by the boardroom of companies: Companies issue new shares to raise more money for future growth. Quite often, in the right industry and under the right leadership, this is a positive move by a company. However, issuing new shares means that anyone holding shares before the issuance will have a less percentage of the overall share of the company than they had previously. This is a form of dilution of assets. The supply of new shares can be increased when the powers at a company feel it is necessary.

The average lifespan of companies is also decreasing over the decades. Competition and the rate of innovation mean that companies must have the ability to introduce new technology or pivot their business to keep up with competition or face going out of business. Companies are not based on code and hard rules. Leaders have to make decisions on the future of the company. CEOs and management teams can change due to bad performance, retirement, or a change of career. New leaders can come in and change the direction of a company for better or worse. Centralised decision-making could make or break a company.

The global Stock market is estimated in **excess of a $100 trillion** market cap in 2022 – could some of the money allocated to the stock market make its way to Bitcoin?

Bitcoin's market cap is currently less than $1 trillion. Gold, which is Bitcoin's closest comparable asset at present, has a market cap in excess of $10 trillion – over 10 times that of Bitcoins market cap. Gold is only one opportunity for Bitcoin to take Market share from. Other than gold, the total market cap of the 3 biggest asset classes mentioned previously, stocks, bonds and real estate, **exceeds $400 trillion** at the time of writing. This means Bitcoin occupies only 0.25% of value of the Total Addressable Market (TAM) for global assets. These assets are over 400 times larger than the Bitcoin asset class. There are also other asset classes that Bitcoin can take a share from like commodities, fine art or collectable cars which people use to store their value over years. The Total Addressable Market of all assets are estimated to be around 900 trillion – 900 times larger than Bitcoins current Value – Without knowing this, many people think they are late to Bitcoin but the asset has magnitudes more room to grow in value.

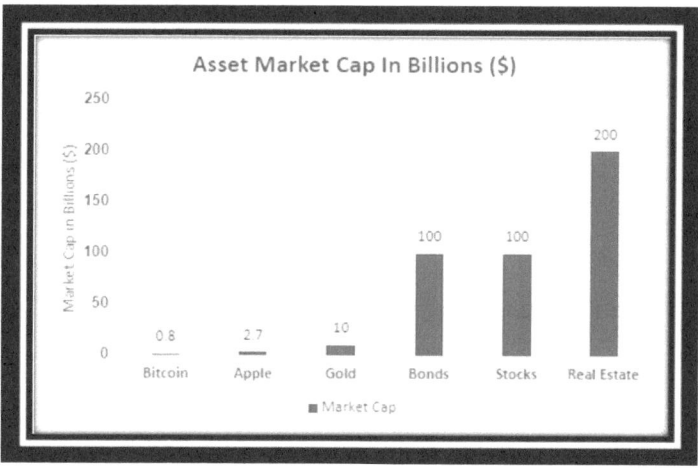

In a world where the adoption of digital technologies is increasing, could Bitcoin consume some of the market cap of traditional asset classes?

What if only 10% of money from these 3 traditional asset classes flowed into Bitcoin, adding over $40 trillion to Bitcoin's market cap – if that were to happen, the price of Bitcoin would be roughly $2 million per Bitcoin.

What if 20% of the money from these assets flowed in to Bitcoin, making Bitcoin $4 million per coin? What if more people start to understand Bitcoin and it is seen as the most trusted, easy to manage investment with huge potential for adoption? What if Bitcoin also becomes a way to exchange money for good and services instead of Fiat currency? What if Bitcoin becomes the main store of value asset class in the world, as well as becoming the world reserve currency where everything globally, like oil and property, is priced in Bitcoin?

Full time profession, Part-time investor: What if money functioned as it should – for example, you save $1000 today and it will purchase you at least the same amount of goods and services in 10, 20, 50 or 100 years from now. Many people are opting for alternative investments as a way of storing purchasing power, knowing that their fiat money today will be worth less in the future.

In the world where money holds its value, investing should only be reserved as a specialist but optional subject.

In a world where money doesn't hold its value, like today, it seems necessary to be an investor. Much of the world is seeking alternatives to store their purchasing power. The dentist, teacher, IT professional, store owner, farmer and many more must not only spend time learning their specialist trade but also spend time to understand the basics of investing, taking them away from improving their own industry.

It's entirely possible that if money returned to its natural state, as neutral money, where the supply cannot be inflated by central banks, people wouldn't need to invest in alternative assets and the money everyone holds can function how it should – **a currency to exchange for goods and services, as well as a method to store value for the future**. The outcome of functioning money should drive down other asset prices as these become less desirable as store of value assets, making things like housing more affordable, while also giving time back to humans to be more productive, who are currently spending time studying and investing in alternative assets in the fiat system world, just to keep up with inflation.

As we wrap up the content on the price and potential future growth of Bitcoin, I want to leave a few facts around Bitcoin scarcity. Scarcity can drive the price upwards. As more investors attempt to secure share of the 21 million Bitcoin the price will increase. The increase in price reinforces the desire to own some Bitcoin. Fear of missing out (FOMO), is a psychological phenomenon in investing whereby people observe their family, friends and peers increasing their wealth through an investment, which leads to more people investing as the price increases. FOMO is not what gives Bitcoin its value but it can lead to explosive price increases, which draws more people to try to understand it, which again increases the adoption as they try to understand more about it.

Let's look at some other interesting facts about Bitcoin as we begin to wrap up:

- According to The Global Wealth Report by Credit Swisse in 2021 there are 56.1 million millionaires by the end of 2020. What if every millionaire wanted to own 1 Bitcoin each – it isn't possible. Millionaires will have to settle for a fraction of a Bitcoin and bid hard if they want to increase their amount of Bitcoin, again driving up the price.

- There are estimated to be around 3-4 million Bitcoin lost forever by people not securing their private keys, particularly in the early days of Bitcoin. The accessible Bitcoin could be as low as 17 million, making Bitcoin even more scarce.

- How to become one of the top 1% of Bitcoin holders? If you divide Bitcoin's 21 million by one percent of the current world population of estimated 7.5 billion, you get 0.28. There are other variables to consider, but holding 0.28 Bitcoin, or

28 million Sats, statistically guarantees you'll be in the top 1% of Bitcoin holders. Keep in mind that there may only be 17 million accessible Bitcoin meaning the number required to be in the top 1% would be even lower than 0.28 Bitcoin.

- May 22nd is known as Bitcoin Pizza Day where an individual in 2010 spent 10,000 Bitcoin, worth around $40 at the time, on 2 Papa John's Pizzas. At the beginning of 2022, 10,000 Bitcoin would be worth an estimated $450+ million. It may be a good idea to start 'stacking Sats' and hold them for 10 years or more.

The adoption of Bitcoin has been in an upward trend every year since the first block was mined. Bitcoin looks to be following the adoption trend of the internet in terms of users. The current adoption rate is comparable to how the internet adoption looked in the late 90's and early 2000's. With the number of wallets increasing, it is projected that Bitcoin will reach 1 billion wallets by 2030, significantly up from an estimated 80 million wallets today. The 1 billion users mark is seen as a significant milestone in technology adoption where the technology becomes a huge part of society and continues to grow as more applications and use cases are discovered. With the adoption rate increasing, the price will inevitably follow.

Bitcoin, in terms of an asset class, is a young adolescent which is volatile in nature but carries enormous potential to grow when compared to other asset classes. It will be interesting to see how fast Bitcoin will be adopted over the coming months, years, and decades and how the price increases alongside adoption.

Summary of Section 4

In this section we looked at how digital and technology adoptions faced resistance in their formative years, and choosing to going along with technology advancements proved to be the successful path. We explored how the properties of Bitcoin compares to gold and how Bitcoin is a digital version of gold. We compared the current fiat system to Bitcoin, where we discovered how the value of fiat currencies are at the mercy of centralized control and have been devalued over many years. We also took a dive in to the Bitcoin price and its key drivers – the inflation of money, the halving and adoption. Finally, we looked at how Bitcoin has the potential to capture market share of traditional assets given its digital properties and simplicity when compared to other assets which make the case for Bitcoin to become the most enticing asset class of the coming decades.

With this book, I set out to take people on a journey to understand how Bitcoin could be one of the most impactful inventions in the history of the world. The key principles are based on understanding money, understanding why Bitcoin was created, and understanding the underlying technology, plus a bonus section called The Emergence of Bitcoin that we hope you found interesting. The book is intended to be thought-provoking and to encourage people to think from first principles and question our current financial systems.

Bitcoin is a simple concept on the surface but has very complex layers as you dive deeper. I hope this book exceeded your expectations. It is intended to educate you on Bitcoin for very reasonable value. Bitcoin has the potential to change and improve the lives of many. I will continue to support the education and adoption of Bitcoin across the world. I hope you continue to learn more from future educational products, where I will further explore the technology, look at some of the contrasting views against Bitcoin and look closely at current and potential future use cases for Bitcoin.

Future content will focus on **Debunking Bitcoin Myths,** such as:

- Bitcoin Energy consumption and how it can incentivize renewable energy.
- Is Bitcoin slow changing technology or is this a feature?
- Is Visa faster than Bitcoin?
- Can a 51% network attack bring down Bitcoin?
- Bitcoin Regulation and the impact on Bitcoin
- Can Bitcoin be banned by Governments?

We will also look at:

- Bitcoin micropayments and the Lightning Network
- Bitcoin Transaction Fees
- Bitcoin as Collateral
- Bitcoin On Chain Analysis – Diving in to the data and activity of the Bitcoin Network
- Bitcoin in 3rd world countries: Banking the unbanked – addressing poverty and access to money
- A Bitcoin circular economy – What if everyone got paid in Bitcoin and spent using Bitcoin?

Plus, much more...

I will continue to bring you more content on Bitcoin. Th[...] you enjoyed this, please leave a review. I'm always ha[...] feedback.

Please pass the book to a friend if you think they will find it us[...]

Additional Reading Material:

Bitcoin.org

Saylor.org

You can follow me on Twitter/X:

@ChrisMc_L

nks again. If
y to hear

ful.

Made in United States
Troutdale, OR
11/03/2025

41233303R00080